Y0-AGH-446

Greetings and Warm Wishes to My Friend

MONTEREY PENINSULA HERALD, DEC. 25, 1989

VERSE

THE PERFECT GIFT

'Tis Christmas time again,
    How quickly passed the year!
I wish you well, Dear Friend
    And toast a cup of cheer.

Auld Lang Syne to you.
    The melody lingers on,
Clasp my hand awhile,
    Hail — and then be gone.

Life has its fleeting moments
    Worldly goods are short delight.
Your friendship is a treasure
    That glows forever bright.

Whitney Latham Lechich

From Your Friend,

WINDMILLS OF OCTOBER

Contemporary Poetry
Volume I

by
WHITNEY LATHAM LECHICH

First Edition
October 1990

WHYS WORLD PUBLICATIONS   PACIFIC GROVE, CA

APOL-OH-GEE!!!

I'd like to think my thoughts as so refined

Thus hoping all the rest will be declined.

So, hie myself to stroll the beach unwind

From suffering beneath oppressive bind;

That gentle breezes lift a guilt inclined

When fact revealed to me my words unkind;

To sadly dim a star once brightly shined

And turn a peaceful brow to furrows lined,

To mar the pleasure being dined and wined.

Now pine for fair one formerly entwined.

So woefully was left, mid fateful grind,

A casualty of windmills of my mind.

In despair I cast about to see what stills

What will tranquilize incessance of windmills.

ACCENT ON THE POSITIVE

A most fortunate person, I
And all who choose to laugh, not cry;
For the world has a way of passing by
    With sadness.

Let's live! Better get on with it!
Life is full of every misfit.
Buffoons are needed to clown a bit
    With laughter.

Everyone has these ups and downs
So, wipe away those furrowed frowns.
Let us all sing, ''Bring in the clowns.''
    With hope.

Just count your blessing one by one.
Say a prayer each day is done.
Greeting the world and rising sun
    With love.

Whitney Latham Lechich

ACHIEVEMENT QUOTIENT*

While driving past the church today,
    Despite Saturday, I saw cars;
A long line, a limousine, a hearse,
    Some soul on its way to the stars.

Scanning the obituary column,
    (What is the present mean on age?)
Many are nipped in the bud
    Without time to become a sage.

Time is a precious commodity;
    Not to be wasted, killed or spent
But hoarded and zealously portioned,
    Lest regret become our lament.

Before we take that long last trip
    An interior journey is in order;
To realize our human potential,
    A quotient for the Great Recorder.

So, dare to dream a noble task,
Your special talent to expound.
If 'tis not completed in this life,
Perhaps, it will, next time around.

*the ratio of achievement age to mental age

ADORATION

I have to be the luckiest person alive,
    To be here, on such a day at ocean's edge;
To be healthy, to be free of cares, to be able
    To absorb this natural wonderland!
What ever have I done to deserve it?
    How can I contribute to this vast
Storehouse of beauty and contentment?
    If only it were possible to package elixir
To give a measure of happiness and sensitivity,
    A share in the exuberance of my heart,
    While bicycling along the oceanside.

Exhilarated by the fresh breezes from the sea,
    Admiring the harmony of burnt orange, juxtaposed
To the dusty-rose of the ice plants in bloom;
    Super-imposed upon the verdant span of fairway,
Crowned by the midnight green of the forest;
    Looking skyward, the expanse of God's canvas,
Splashed with crimson sunset over an azure sky;
    Blending, dissolving into the blue-green sea,
Alive and restless with undulating, foaming sprays,
    The epitome of eternal life and beauty
And profoundly, I feel at one with my Creator.

[4]

AFFINITY FOR THE STARS

I've related to the stars
From the time I was small,
My eyes searched the skies
With affinity for all.

Knowing an innocent thrill
When the heavens were bright
Love and communion above
In the still of the night.

Basking in their splendor
Feeling the stars akin,
A longing and belonging
Sensing our oneness within.

My soul the stuff of stars!
Erect, my head held high
Never, a lone night ever
When I can see the sky.

BORN ASTRIDE PEGASUS*

I feel a kinship, stars related to me

From recent scientific analysis

Now, I comprehend this affinity.

Only stars were hot enough in the abyss,

A particle solely capable of creating

The chemicals of man's constitution.

Through this ancient astral our relating

Man became the stuff of star solution.

Small wonder aviators escape the earth,

Feel unbounded joy, embrace the sky

With the freedom felt of a child at birth;

No woes or fears to conflict, confine, deny

    Their souls, — unlimited by worldly bars

    Climb heavenward, at home there in the stars.

*PEGASUS, winged horse of Greek mythology, symbol of poetic inspiration

BETRAYED

By whose womb shall this child be known;
By the woman who produced the egg?
By the woman whose body accepted the embryo?
From the woman in whose heart it was to beg
The glory of motherhood from a total stranger;
By the woman so desperate to hold a child,
Never knowing her trust was frought with danger.
The woman whose spouse was willing to pay;
Using his sperm to create their child,
Eagerly awaiting the event day after day.
Solomon, in his wisdom a child would not divide,
The future of four people, courts must decide;
    This hireling now claims a mother's right
    Even though black and the child is white.

Oct. 22, 1990, it was announced that the court had awarded
sole custody to the genetic parents.

MINI POETRY SESSION

Meter represents rhythm in poetry.
Two syllables equal one foot. Poems are composed of a certain
number of feet per line. Some poems are very specific as to
the number of lines — syllables — meter and also the number
of rhyme sounds and exactly where they are placed.

FRENCH FORM   THE TRIOLET

has 4 feet to the line

8 lines only

2 rhyme sounds only

Repetitions in lines 1 - 4 -7

The 8th line is the same as the 2nd.

EXAMPLE

I saw the sign of "Cats at Play,"	1.	a	①	
While walking down a shady road.	2.	b	②	b
To me, it seemed so weird to say	3.	a		
If, however true, "Cats at Play."	4.	a	④	
So I proceeded on my way	5.	a		
Into their territory strode.	6.	b		
To my dismay, found cats at play.	7.	a	⑦	
While walking down a shady road.	8.	b	⑧	b

CATASTROPHIC DILEMMA

Death will not find me lying idle and waiting
Wracked with cruel disease that fell to my lot,
For I signed the paper the world found debating;
To pull the plug, or 'tis nobler to let men rot.
Once health and zest are gone with my mobility
And years have piled high on the weathered side;
Without desire and approaching senility,
On visit full quota, no longer wish to reside;
To remain as spectacle, a testing tube in case!
Have a yearn to return to my home in the sky,
Leaving room for another to take my place.
So, please God, I pray the dignity to quietly die
    As I have plans for my future next time around.
    The soul of me will never be found —
        underground.

THE CUTTING EDGE

More to be pitied than envied
  Those whose careers are on clock- race.
A ballplayer's time runs out faster,
  Than he does while making first base.

The actor's time of prime is fickle,
  To be adored for a few short seasons.
Then shelved for all eternity;
  Forever bearing the lesions.

The contractor who bids for jobs,
  Lives in a precarious atmosphere,
Making it big or losing his shirt;
  He never knows from year to year.

I've heard a postal clerk complain,
  Monotony of the job drives him berserk.
He earns a wage year in and year out,
  With security, no lack of work.

Some toil hard to make a living;
Some strive to make a pile.
All have something to complain about,
  It seems to be the style.
  Man is a curious creature.
What he DOESN'T HAVE is the wedge,
 It keeps him unstable, living on
  THE CUTTING EDGE

Whitney Latham Lechich

DANDELIONS ARE FOREVER

Sad to say, during a drought
flowers cherished have perished
planted seeds come to naught,
hardly the garden you had sought.
But should you go away
for a fortnight and a day,
return and you'll find
Dandelions in full array.

Not the unintrusive flat ones
but waist high multi-facet ones
with twenty puffs on each prong
until a wind might come along.
Anyone would rather be a bard
than do the weeding in the yard.
While they grow anywhere
some people have a greater share.

No wonder in lands over seas
they say, ''Pass the dandelions, please.''
So devour them with good reason
a tasty snack with proper season.
They were well named dande-LION
In a field they are the scion.
When God said, ''Go forth and multiply.''
He must have had a mote* within His eye.

*mote, sawdust, a speck of dust. Biblical: ''He who would censor others must first remove the mote from his own eye.'' Matthew 7:3 and Luke 6:41

DECISIONS

Though I were to travel this world
    Over many times and more
Till I knew by heart the by-ways
Of hill and lane, I'd still remain
    Standing at the door.

Childhood is blissfully unaware
    Adolescence without care
But with maturity has arisen
Necessity for decisions and I am
    Standing at the door.

Only the brave dare to enter,
    The answer is there for all
But knowledge is a heavy chore;
    With this thought in mind
    I'm standing at the door.

If I force myself to decide,
    Lift the latch and go inside;
Ready for the task before
Maybe I could help the next one
    Who is standing at the door.

DECLARATION

Here I come, as I am, ready or not
Over the wall, jumping in with both feet,
Invading cloistered circles you have wrought.
Leave it to me, not often too discreet.

When one gets on in years measured ingot*,
To make your mark in a time when we are living,
You must say what is thought before it's forgot;
What your life is about, the reason for being.

It can't be helped, meaning toes are tread on,
There's no time for pussy-footing around.
I have message with light to be shed upon
Open minds, of those who do not astound;
    For I'm not so tame as to play their game,
    I'm pinch-hitting for gadfly**, in Socrates' name.

*ingot: a measurement of gold.

**gadfly: 1. horsefly 2. a person who goads or irritates others; as
      Socrates referred to himself.

DEER SEASON

There's a road along the ocean,
　　Green fairway the other side,
There's a feeling of eternity
　　With space so open wide.
The sky is pure with clarity
　　Like best of agéd wine.
The air is filled with fragrance
　　From saplings of the pine.

The birds are gliding up above
　　On a current in the sky.
A perfect splendid summer day
　　With tourists driving by.
A crowd is parked along the road.
　　A camera frenzy here?
No, just an everyday occurrence,
　　Taking pictures of the deer.

But, the deer are quite alert,
　　Ears pricked up high like that!
You can see their puzzled faces;
　　What are tourists staring at?
Briefly, they do a people-watch,
　　It interrupts their grazing.
Then, soon lose interest, as people
　　Are not all that amazing.

DÉJÀ VU

I'm a child of the Universe
  Born with a cord 'round my neck,*
Destined to reach greater heights
  Beyond what, even I, expect.

This affinity for the world,
  My need to travel is a vow.
I feel a presence in these souls,
  Of their God, to whom I bow.

Examining things of yesteryear,
  Picking them over like a vulture,
Searching the remnants of history
  For clues from a long lost culture.

Some shabby relic of the past
  May be a treasure in my eyes,
Imbued with fragments of glory,
  A spirit that never dies.

I have traveled this road before,
  So much of it is déjà vu.
Who, what, where, when and why?
  I wish I knew — I wish I knew!

*It is often fatal when a child is born with the umbilical cord around the neck,
therefore when they live they are considered to have a special destiny.

[15]

DON'T HOVER OVER EACH OTHER

A Rule-of-the House with my Spouse.
Share if you like — hobby or sport
But not of necessity that could abort
The fragile communion of a good union.
When building love it's important to know
The art of leaving some "room to grow."

Hold hands in public places,
Never mind incredulous faces.
They really envy your Special Thing,
The love in your eyes and a wedding ring.
Knowing there'll be times you don't agree
Adds spice to life realistically.

Begin and end each day with a kiss;
Lower defenses when things go amiss,
So each can "save face" if there's been a blunder;
Create understanding, not naive wonder.
Be each other's champion on the bottom line,
Then none can put asunder Your Valentine!

EQUAL TIME

The papers are full of misdemeanors,
 Glorifying bums with short fuse,
'Twould be great to read about the good guys
 With equal time in the daily news.

Are we waiting until our world becomes
 So evil that evil is thought the norm?
Are we waiting until we hit the bottom
 Before turning the cheek of reform?

Give an example — a hero, if you will.
 There are plenty around that are unsung;
But, noble deeds don't get the equal time
 And youth needs heroes to walk among.

No one can expect didactic papers, but
 Circulation would increase, be widely read
With some equal time to report the winners;
 Not just a crime after crime instead.

Support these parents who have set an example
 To endow a child with a bit of spine;
To think of their bodies as special gifts;
 So, make news of their endeavors with
 EQUAL TIME.

EULOGY TO EMILY D.

A gentle wraith with manner mild,
   most talented of spirit child;
   she haunted summer's garden lees
   and softly whispered to the bees
   as they were flitting to and fro
   to help her lovely flowers grow.

All dressed in white for day and night,
   she wrote in stealth by candle light
   with verse so tender about the bees
   did not reveal they were the keys
   to learn of her wistful loneliness
   with mystery clues for none to guess.

She wrote and hid her poems of love,
   no prayer was answered from above;
   did leave this world with broken heart,
   a saddened recluse torn apart
   behind the curtains of sheerest lace
   a song was sung with words of grace.

Born Dec. 10, 1830, in Amherst, Mass.; died May 5, 1886.
First Book of poems was published posthumously in 1890.

[18]

TO FLEE OR NOT TO FLEA

I dreamed I had a puppy dog
    That was so fond of me,
I could not sit for anytime
    Without his paw upon my knee.

His eyes were dark and soulful
    And pleaded tenderly,
Could you spare a little time
    To come and play with me?

He would even stop his eating
    If I showed signs of fun.
He quivered with anticipation,
    In hopes we'd take a run.

Of course I could not go,
    Whenever friends would roam.
I had to pass up invitations,
    To feed a dog at home.

He'd chew my clothes till dawn,
    Then find something to bark at!
Pleased as punch, he left his mark
    When he piddled on the carpet.

So my dream dog won't come true,
    Sure of this; I'm not ready yet.
I'll compromise with a ceramic dog,
    And a fur coat — to pet.

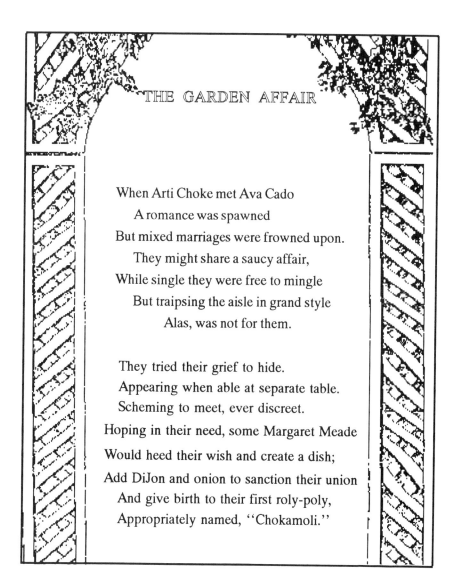

THE GARDEN AFFAIR

When Arti Choke met Ava Cado
  A romance was spawned
But mixed marriages were frowned upon.
  They might share a saucy affair,
While single they were free to mingle
  But traipsing the aisle in grand style
    Alas, was not for them.

They tried their grief to hide.
Appearing when able at separate table.
Scheming to meet, ever discreet.
Hoping in their need, some Margaret Meade
Would heed their wish and create a dish;
Add DiJon and onion to sanction their union
  And give birth to their first roly-poly,
  Appropriately named, "Chokamoli."

THE GUEST (GUESS) ROOM

There's a window that won't open,
　　The bed is covered with sewing;
A machine in the far corner,
　　The closet is overflowing.
There are boxes stacked around,
　　A suitcase here and there;
With ironing board in this corner,
　　But, as a bedroom, it's a spare.

So, do come and visit with us.
　　Please overlook the lint.
It's okay for one night only,
　　(Hoping you'll take the hint.)
If your plan is for longer than this,
Of a cold I've symptoms coming down
And know you'll find more comfort
　　At a hotel somewhere in town!

THE HAPPY CRICKET

Though in hiding, I hear your call
    And take it personally,
While I know it's not to me
    You would communicate.
That chirp made by your legs
    Is really calling for a mate.

I admire the wisdom of the Oriental
    Who treasure a cricket, albeit,
Installed in a tiny cage ornamental,
    They consider it a household pet.

I never sought this little friend,
    Dwelling twenty years without him.
Before we sold he came to dwell
    And I was delighted about him,
Furthermore, glad when accidental,
    He moved along to our rental.

Often wondering what he ate —
    To keep him healthy sans a mate?
It may be just a useless quirk
    But I worry about his feed
For when I hear his happy chirp,
    It nourishes me and fills my need.

HEROES NEEDED

Ballplayers aren't heroes
They're just playing a game
That they are well paid for.
It isn't just the same
As if they did something
Brave, without a reward.

Such as fight for clean air,
Influence kids against drugs.
There'd be a point to collect cards
With pictures of their mugs.
The same goes for movie stars
Though some champion good causes.

If you happen to be famous
For whatever reason,
Use your name to endorse,
By inspiring our youth
To set their course
For clean living.

If you never do another thing
That alone will suffice
To put some kid
Back on the track
Who's fallen off once or twice
And needs a hand up.

HOME BY THE BAY

When I was young, still in my teens,
I fashioned a future out of dreams
Conjured from some poems I'd read,
And things that other people said.

I'd like to have a house within
The sound and smell of surf and sea
Where lonesome fog came creeping in
Shrouding the land in mystery.

While I was only visiting then
I solemnly vowed to come again
To live by the bay in Monterey
And here is where I live today!

Though I roam the state and nation
I feel the same, though older now,
Can say without trepidation
I'll always return to keep my vow.
This is my home and this I know,
I shall return where'er I go.

IDENTITY MANDALA

Life is full of compromise
  which makes the joy more keen
  I surmise
  than constant pursuit of heart's desire,
  as steady diet would soon tire
  the most voracious appetite.

Doing one's duty at mundane things,
  snatching precious moments
  often brings
  sheer delight in a hobby diverse;
  or exotic lands to traverse
  tempted by a rainbow.

Sad for those who never escape,
  who never by mind nor body
  partake,
  the soundless call of distant lands
  the urge to learn from history
  what existed before the "ME."

Knowing and learning from the past
  creates an identity that is vast;
  relating to many customs unique,
  absorbing them, to then immerse
  a child of the Universe!

IN THE IMAGE OF GOD

In the landscape of the brain there is
    A fundamental unit cell called a neuron,
"The aristocrat," among the structures of the body.
    There are billions of neurons in the brain.
When this system goes awry, incurable disease
    Steals moments, memory and rational thought.
The cortex governs thought, memory and sensation.
    Sympathetic nerves signal flight or fight.

It is the most delicate, intricate system imaginable
    And yet, fighters pummel each other's heads,
Alcoholics dull the activity of their brains.
    Today's use of chemicals destroys, forever
The unique possibilities of the brain's function.
    Diseases that men contract carelessly
Can toll the bell on what might have been;
    Being born with potential to reach great heights,
To peruse the writings of geniuses of all times;
    We willingly, knowingly, annihilate this holy gift!
    For it is in this intelligence, that we are made
    In the image of God.

With the free will to become an angel or
    to become an animal.

IN OUR TIME

In our time
>Supplications are wafted heavenward
>Hope, is an aura hovering above this world
>That's beginning to see the dove.

In our time
>A prayer for World Democracies is said
>Where all can arbitrate their differences
>Without senseless wars and needless bloodshed.

In our time
>War weary nations yearn for peace, each vies
>To sit at the same table to negotiate,
>To strive for compromise.

In our time
>Crimes consigned in the name of nationalism
>May their weapons be forged to plow-shares
>May food hush the children's cries in this chasm.

In our time
>The anguish of man's short lived mortality
>With all the same hopes, need essentially,
>Dear God, let this dream become a reality —

In our time, ONE WORLD!

KNOCK, KNOCK

If you knock before I comb my hair, I'll be there.
If you come when my feet are bare, I'll be there —
 But there is one thing I can't abide
 And will always run and hide,
 Never invite you to come inside
 When I feel naked!
I don't mean Mother Nature in disguise —
 It's only when my eyes
 Are not made-up to tantalize,
 I feel as bald as an old coot
 And naked as my birthday suit!
You can knock all day, I don't give a hoot.
 I'M NOT THERE!

JUDICIAL REPRIEVE

Joan of Arc, for witchcraft was burned at the stake,
 500 year later, canonized as a saint.
Said of the "Maid of Orleans" they'd made a mistake
 Because she wore pants thought she was quaint!
On a horse she gallantly rode into the fray
 With banners unfurled she led the way.
By some, she was a French woman greatly adored
 Who challenged the English in the name of the Lord.

LEFT OUT

She sat there at
    the head of the stair
    in her rocking chair.

She had command
    of all her land
    from the veranda.

The skin of her hand
    thin and shriveled
    with veins expelled.

The hair of her head
    as white as snow
    formed a halo.

Her eyes peered out
    clear and alert
    did not avert.

But, her mind did ponder
    those loved the best
    were all now at rest.

'Twas lonely being the only
    One out of seven
    Left out of Heaven.

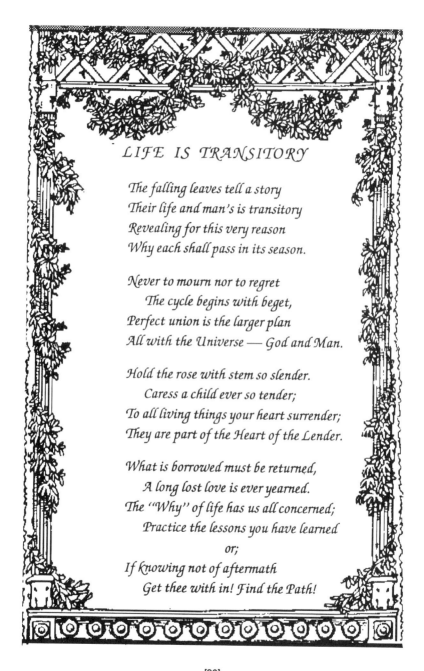

LIFE IS TRANSITORY

The falling leaves tell a story
Their life and man's is transitory
Revealing for this very reason
Why each shall pass in its season.

Never to mourn nor to regret
   The cycle begins with beget,
Perfect union is the larger plan
All with the Universe — God and Man.

Hold the rose with stem so slender.
   Caress a child ever so tender;
To all living things your heart surrender;
They are part of the Heart of the Lender.

What is borrowed must be returned,
   A long lost love is ever yearned.
The "Why" of life has us all concerned;
   Practice the lessons you have learned
      or;
If knowing not of aftermath
   Get thee with in! Find the Path!

THE LONELY ROAD

Walking the lonely road
  in search of a fellow traveler.
  Under the trestle camp fires aglow
  there was wine to share long ago;
But man ages wearing seven league boots,
yearns to settle and establish roots.

Willing to work for a woman's keep,
    fancies a warm body near to sleep;
    someone to join at days end
    with intimacy more than a friend;
    to count on her as one you own,
    working together to build a home.
To create a new life in more ways than one
'till the fruit of your union begets a son.
    Now, as a family you belong
    to an ever increasing mutual throng.

A society that has earned necessities
now, strives to embrace the amenities
    as books, written by men of sight
    expanding desire of mind and might;
    and noble books on the Golden Rule,
    along with classics taught in school
    so, man has now come full circle.
He saw his need and thus learned to live,
    a debt he owes for such a miracle
    is a part of himself which he must give.

  Seeing in the distance on the lonely road
    another traveler who carries no load;
  Speak to him of burdens that enhance a being,
  of the road and the search of the Golden Mean.

[31]

LOVE TOKEN

If you would give me a gift
make it one of doing
with your arm-about my waist
not in a manner wooing.
But in friendship spend your time,
when distant write a letter,
make a sincere effort to
get to know me better.
Send no gifts because the day
dictates a gift in order,
but a gesture fond and true
binding friendship with a mortar —
ever strong and ever lasting
an expression of your esteem,
by telephone or verse on cards,
by sentiments that pass between —
two persons who have respect;
who exchange confidence with trust.
This kind of gift is worth our time.
Give the other to someone else,
if you must.

A MERE WORD

Love — is a word, no more, no less,
    Yet, I thusly you address.
Can it contain a throbbing heart,
    A flame that sets the world apart?

Who be these mortals that maintain
    Rapture will a word contain?
What then remains for humble one,
    Who wishes joy beneath the sun?

How inadequate the word is then
    To be repeated again and again
Yet, in no way can it express
    The song supreme of happiness.

But as the custom was begun
    Just who am I to be undone?
So, here and now to the one I woo,
    I say, "My Darling, I LOVE YOU."

THE MACHINE AGE

There is a friend of whom I'm fond;
    I phoned to invite for a visit.
But her machine said she is out —
    Please leave a message, "Who is it?"

So, I talk to this machine (feeling the fool)
    saying when and where I'm calling from.
Like a kid recites in school;
    With a friendly "Goodbye" when I am done.

    Then, back to my chores, washing hair
        Tops the list, and when soaking wet
    The phone rings, wouldn't you know!
        My friend, returning the call, I bet!
    But I'm impervious, like a queen —
        (Continue washing) letting HER
        TALK TO MY MACHINE.

MAN-CHILD

In stocking feet he measures six feet tall,
Physically strong, yet born with half a brain.
The biggest mistake-maker of them all,
Not sense enough to come out of the rain.
But don't put him down as he won't give up,
Not resting on his laurels to watch T.V.
He always strives to find what he can 'whup;'
He smiles like a child, ever so sweetly.
For nothing ventured, nothing gained
And one doesn't count a fail who hasn't tried.
The effort he made has been sustained;
True, this was his boast just before he died,
    That he challenged life — the learning quest
    Mistakes or no, — he always did his best!

NECTAR OF THE GODS

Men can be like animal trainers who crack the whip.

Ladies making their own decisions are too bold.

Females on leash are allowed small freedoms to sip,

Then cowed to submit; to do as they are told.

Any step out of line, a penalty would enfold.

Women have brains to study more than 'kitchen sink';

Have need to grow up, not merely grow old.

How break this link? Nectar of Equality, they must drink.

Learn this courage to speak up, if needs be, retract;

Not be servants, but persons entitled to aspire;

Not to be cornered, losing sight of the fact

To rise above man's self-centeredness and desire;

    To become more than kittens with unopened eyes,

    Thus their destiny in the universe to realize.

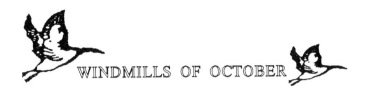

WINDMILLS OF OCTOBER

High upon the hill standing silently and still
Not stirred by distant breezes far at sea,
Stately and tall lording over all, the old windmill.

Then blasted from the north of late December's chill
'Twas shrouded in drifted snow there upon the lee,
High upon the hill standing silently still.

April brought the rains with whistling winds so shrill;
Wild birds flight silhouette the coming of the night,
Stately and tall lording over all, the old windmill.

Summer's gentle south wind flirted leaves so tranquil,
The flowers faded after invaded by the roving bee.
High upon the hill standing silently and still.

But October days lift the haze windblown from the sea.
They clear the mind and start the grind of machinery
High upon the hill — no longer silently and still,
Stately and tall lording over all, spins the old windmill.

THE OTHER GUY

The other guy stays out of trouble,
    His name isn't in the news.
The other guy doesn't play ball
    Games, are not for him to choose.

The other guy may be a book worm.
    Having two jobs to work
To finish his education,
    Can't hang around and shirk.

The other guy may help his folks
    With the necessities of life,
He can't afford a racy car,
    His only hope, a working wife.

So, he goes his plodding way,
    No paper prints his worth.
These guys are the real heroes
    Veritably, the salt of the earth.

For a hero is not the guy
    Acting on the spur of the moment;
But the one who's diligent day by day
    Praise him, for he is Heaven sent!

A POCKET FULL OF WRY

Displayed there upon the mantle,
(Chagrined when I saw the dust,)
On the nic-nacks over the years
That I once had deemed a "must."

Was it Shakespeare who once said,
"All is vanity?" I thought
At one time a strange remark
And so, I bought and bought.

Now, I no longer feed my vanity
But go to auctions as I travel,
Seeing remnants of other lives
Sold for a pittance under the gavel.
It is hoped that sometime in life
Wisdom is acquired with age.
Perhaps, now I understand
The obscure words of that sage.

I am now content just to look
I no longer need to acquire.
I've lost my "possessiveness"
And treasure a pleasure to admire.

THE SHELL GAME

Put this shell to your ear,
    Hold your breath and listen.
Tell me what it is you hear
    While iridescence glisten.

Could sound emit from overseas
    Or denizens of the deep?
The wonder of it sure to please
    Is a treasure rare to keep.

Now to dream is pure delight
    Enhancing every mood.
Cultivate that fancy flight
    When you're done with childhood.

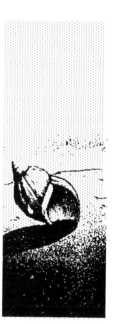

Whenever life is sorely pressed
    And efforts seem in vain,
Recall a virtue truly blessed
    To once more play this game.

POETRY

Poetry is like the shell
Hold it to your eye or ear
Tell me what it is you hear
That brings a silent tear.

Poetry pours out your heart
Transports you near or far;
Friend of understanding dreams
Reaching for a star.

A sudden burst of laughter
Then a solemn pensive look
Smiles will gently fade away
When you've closed the book.

QUINTESSENCE*

Man needs AIR to breath

FIRE for warmth and a mate;

WATER to cleanse and nourish

This EARTH to inseminate.

Of these four elements there is no doubt,

One more thing man can't live without

All others above, he needs SOUL** to love.

*SOUL is the fifth essence, the ultimate substance,
purest, most perfect manifestation; therefore,
the QUINTESSENCE.

**Anthony Damiani, author, *Looking Into Mind* (d. 1984) was called "a truly great man" by the Dalai Lama. Damiani says, "We are the mind....experience of this mind...you experience your own soul. You are soul."

MINI RANIVILLA SESSION

Having nine lines of limited syllables and three rhyme
  sounds as indicated:

Syllables	rhymes	line	rhymes
4		1	
4		2	# 1 rhyme sound
6		3	
6		4	
7		5	
6	# 2 rh. sound	6	#3 rhyme sound
4		7	
4		8	
6		9	

EXAMPLE

CHIANTI

Our grapes so sweet
none could compete,
The fairest of the field.
In vineyards they do twine
hanging ripe upon the vine,
a bumper crop will yield.
To make such fine,
full-bodied wine
laws are since repealed.

SOMETHING FOR EVERYONE

Carmel-by-the-Sea is as quaint as it can be,
Little houses behind big trees; small hotels, aim to please.

Given directions you must write down,
For there are no numbers in the town.
Third from the corner on the right going north,
Enjoy yourself, as you sally forth.

You'd think writing a letter to no avail
But all go to the P.O. for their mail.
While inconvenient at times it's true,
You could also greet the friends you knew.

Bakeries and boutiques there are many,
Art galleries in every nook and cranny.
There are sandy beaches to allure;
And cars of Continental Concours.
The Back festival and the Mission are distingué,
Also good theatre and dining gourmét.

So, we're off to Carmel for a lark,
Knowing full well it's hard to park;
But compared to the city and high-rise
This village, is a veritable Paradise.
So, come and enjoy before it, too, dies,
Choked with people up to the eyes!

Or. . I should say, stay away, let me advise,
For I have told you lies, lies, lies, lies!

SHADOWS IN THE CAVES YET

O, I've been criticized to some extent
As always one is who ventures out-of-line.
Some would deign to call enthusiasm brash
And modesty is hardly a virtue of mine.
All second-hand collections would be trash;
And one who speaks up, be notoriety bent.
But nought gets done by shrinking violet
Thus one who sounds a voice and yields a pen
Justly deserves the heroes metal and honor.
For peace will not derive from cannon ween*
But more oft by those who forge and donor,
Not blood to spurt from eye-ball as yet to let,
    To quell their woes and seemingly their foes
    But by God's intelligence, all sanity knows.

*ween (wèn): to think, suppose, imagine.

SONO CONTENTO*

I stood on the mountain alone
looking at the valley below,
With wind blowing through my hair.
What a wonderful feeling 'twas
    Just to be standing there.

I turned and faced the sun
Streaming from the heavens above;
Seeing mist from the mountain rise
And all the glories of earth,
    Displayed before my eyes.

I followed a narrow trail
'Twas scarred with the print of hoofs.
having only an hour to spare,
I wondered what had beckoned?
    What was I doing there?

The air was filled with such peace,
Only laws of nature ruled
Little creatures in hurry bent
Ignoring me, scurried past
    And I was content.

*SONO CONTENTO (ITALIAN): I am content.

TASHIZAN*

Entering autumn of our years,
    Slide gently forth the abacus,
Lest recrimination and our tears
    May cast a shadow back on us.

This should be our Golden Age, the
    Culmination of dreams realized;
Acknowledging human frailties
    With love and understanding eyes.

To only count ensuing years
    Rational life goes down the drain.
Unless you gather sweet memories
    Marking time is all in vain.

Never take this life for granted.
    To be catered to and courted;
But treat it as treasure borne,
    Lest its spirit be aborted.

*TASHIZAN (JAPANESE): to sum it up; the addition

TIMES HAVE CHANGED

Once upon a time you could tell
The girls from the boys by the the way they dressed.
But times have changed, that's the reason I guessed.
It's not the same. Times have changed.

Now, you're taking a chance
With a hasty glance at a pair of pants.
So, hair became a clue, you couldn't misconstrue;
During a certain milieu. But times have changed;
Today, they're both askew!

Time was you could trust an earring.
Who else would wear such a thing? —
Short of being a ding-a-ling? But times have changed.
You'd think he'd be adverse and only SHE
Would carry a purse, but times have changed!

For awhile, the Mohawk haircut was in style.
As if that wasn't totally obtuse,
Then, they colored it chartreuse!
What matches is out, the odd-ball has the clout.
Every exasperated parent admits,
Kids, today, are really THE PITS!
AND TIMES HAVE CHANGED.

TIME MARCHES ON

I think I'm coming unglued,
  It makes me feel like a dunce
As strange things are happening
  Surreptitiously, not at once
But little by little I notice
  Unusual embarrassments occur.

Where once I could hear a pin drop
  You, now, have to yell in my ear.
I recall when my eyes were 20/20.
  To see a hair was no stint
Now, with glasses on I peer into
  Even the largest print.

  I like to think I'm wiser
  In some way to compensate;
But I keep forgetting what day it is
  Arriving too soon or too late.
  But compared to my peers
  I still have years,
There's something that hasn't diminished
My appetite's strong, hasn't gone wrong,
  When I lose THAT, — I'm finished!

TRAVELING COMPANION

He who sees his lady faire
    As a lass with flowing hair.
Plump of cheek with rosy glow,
    Light of step and on the go.
May well enjoy them while they last
But find more treasures when they're past.

For twilight on the silvery hair
    Of one who once, was oh, so fair
Forms halo around withered cheek
    May still enshrine the soul you seek
Whose presence now, exceeds all wealth;
Whose proferred hand is grace itself.

For God's great plan when he made men,
    Intelligence, bestowed on them
That through each other they might find
    Eternal love and peace of mind;
Without credence, the fickle heart
    Oft' infatuated is torn apart.

Man has passions not to trust
    Over which, with will he must
Control them and his heart as well.
    Choosing a companion to ring the bell
And chart the course which he must plod
    On his journey back to God.

TRILOGY

PENSO
(I THINK)

My mind is an open book
Should I read today? I muse,
Or perhaps, just refuse.
    And let it go astray
    On its merry way'
    Adopt a wait-and-see,
    Out of curiosity.

SENTO
(I FEEL)

This morning when I awoke,
    Of luck, I had a stroke.
Not a stroke debilitating,
    But one most exhilarating.

I felt like a lamb in spring,
    Cavorting around to do my thing.
Chores were done, that I might say,
    Not put-off for another day!

CREDO
(I BELIEVE)

I feel that I've been singularly blessed,
For I think of my mind as a treasure chest.

To be able to recall yester-year,
Is truly an emerald without peer.
    The present
is filled with all sorts of stuff.
It's like a diamond in the rough,
Every facet creates brilliance,
Exploding light and resilience.
    The future
is mine to design, the shaping
Is like a pearl in the making.

Jewels or junk, a coin is tossable,
If you believe, all things are possible.

UNREQUITED LOVE

There's a time when gentle lovers will tackle,
Escaping from a world where hope has fled.
Daring the grisly concept of death, unshackle;
To mourn an unrequited love, now dead;
For whom, if still were living, wouldn't turn a hair.
Revealed in the light of infinite tomorrows,
Would avoid with struggle, repugnant to bear.
In a life mundane of sharing duty and sorrows,
Lost would be, the rare glow of the unique;
To losing its bloom in time worn-out fashion
Escalating moments of rapture peake
As flame consuming, early, yearning passion;
    Instead, an ideal in the ravage of time expire,
    Will forever be, ashes of roses left on the pyre.

UP, UP AND AWAY!

From coast to coast without a care
    Now, the celebrity flies.
Rich and famous who must be there
    Take to the friendly skies.
MGM Grand, a very small airline,
    Customized Boeing 727;
Will cater to you, wine and dine
    Gourmet food close to heaven.

Twice a day in each direction,
    $2,000 dollars, N.Y. to L.A.
It's the stand-up bar connection
    Across the U.S.A.
To go aboard without a horde
    Not even carry a duffle;
To while the hours on whiskey sours
    Or perhaps, a chocolate truffle.

For service like this you pay a price
    But are treated royally
Protected from mobs not always nice;
    Flying with friends, socially.
Oh, to be a celebrity
    It's my secret desire,
To meet Robin Leach in reality
    And to be a 'frequent flyer.'

VANGUARD OF THE CENTURY
TRIBUTE TO GORBACHEV

Out of the Phoenix* of suspicion and distrust
    A man of the people extends a new lease
Our arch enemy has become our friend;
    Hope is brewing now for World Peace.**

This simple, honest leader of a nation
    Caused walls to come down, unity restored.
Leads his people on the path of glasnost
    Curtails his military might, now stored.

His perseverance in the sight of opposition;
    His diplomacy, humor and feist,
Is doubted by incredulous war mongers
    Of the same ilk that crucified Christ.

Why are we always such "doubting Thomases?"
    Skeptical of good but not of evil?
The world has known war and rumors of wars
    All instigated by himself, the Devil.

It is the first time a leader has talked Peace,
    putting his military might on the line.
Let's pray some trigger-happy radical doesn't
    Queer our chances for Peace in Our Time.

*Phoenix, Egyptian mythical bird that rose from the ashes to renewed life.

**October 15, 1990, President Gorbachev was awarded
the Nobel Peace Prize.

WOUNDED

When hospitality or ego are trampled on,
You hold your tongue of manners well in-bred;
Yet, mutely mull this incident upon
Harsh were words to fall upon your head.
Let's be fair, admonishing yourself,
Don't expect too much from those too young.
Embroiled, in drama of adolescence theirself,
Like a yo-yo on string suspended strung,
Taunt to twang at slightest provocation;
Pretend a wisdom that fluctuates by day,
Not heeding gleanings of prior generation;
Not seeing a broader perspective but may
    Later, relate the yarn where they did chaff
    In ridiculous manner as to make you laugh.

X-AMPLE

X in mathematics is an unknown quantity
    But has many meanings more than this.

X is the signature of those who cannot write;
    From one who can, it sends a kiss.

X with bars (=) is a Bo Dereck Roman ten.
    X chromosome determines sex of offspring.

X marks the spot where the body was found;
    X-ray is taking pictures of everything. . .

Your "X" referred to a "has-been number one."
    That's XXX* for tonight and fini for this pun!

*"30" the signoff signal for broadcasting

YOUNG LOVE:

SO BE IT

Alas, this emotional turmoil is distracting,

Descending into quiet pools, disturbs reflections;

Bowing down these many years of silver headed grey

To bear witness the anguish of one and twenty —

Rebirths, those own heart-rending days of yore

When torn apart by indecision, God, what agony!

Now, with remembrance mirrored in this lonely child;

Incapable of sparing her an hour of suffering,

For none have ears so deaf nor eyes so blind

As those who bask in the drama of lovesickness.

All attempts of consolation are cast aside

Her grief is precious and coddled to run its course.

  Save your breath, waste not a moments dissuasion

    To mourn is her birthright and she has chosen to do so.

ZIS EES ZE LEEMIT

If you haven't found a poem
    that relates to you
Send me a postcard, I'll see
    what I can do.

But let me say here,
    in case you mistook
I hope you enjoyed
    reading my first book.

Sincerely yours,   First Edition # 000279

12-26-90

Whitney Latham Lechick

WHYS WORLD PUBLICATION
P. O. BOX 51235
PACIFIC GROVE, CA 93950
To re-order: Single copy $8.00 plus $1.00 handling fee.
For three gift copies $21.00 plus $2.00 handling.
For hard bound cover add $4.00 to the above for each book.
Please allow two weeks for mailing.
Offer expires Jan. 1, 1992

[58]

INDEX